Digging Canadian History

Digging Canadian History

by Rebecca L. Grambo

WALRUS
B O O K S

Edited by Ben D'Andrea
Design and illustration by Five Seventeen/ PicaPica.ca

Printed and bound in Canada.

LIBRARY AND ARCHIVES CANADA CATALOGUING IN PUBLICATION
Grambo, Rebecca, 1963–
Digging Canadian history/ Rebecca Grambo.

Includes index.
ISBN 1-55285-757-3
978-1-55285-757-1

1. Canada—Antiquities—Juvenile literature.
2. Anthropology—Canada—Juvenile literature.
3. Natural history—Canada—Juvenile literature.
4. Canada—History—Juvenile literature. I. Title.

FC172.G69 2006   j971.01   C2005-906773-X

The publisher acknowledges the support of the Canada Council and the Cultural Services Branch of the Government of British Columbia in making this publication possible. Whitecap Books also acknowledges the financial support of the Government of Canada through the Book Publishing Industry Development Program for our publishing activities.

Photograph and Illustration Acknowledgements

8–9 C. Arnold/Prince of Wales Northern Heritage Centre (detail) 12–13 Illustration by Five Seventeen 14 Parks Canada/1977/H.01.11.06.09(45) (detail) 17 Parks Canada/ Shane Kelly/1998 19 Parks Canada/Archaeological Collections Management/24M1335T (detail) 20 The Burial at L'Anse Amour, illustration by Steve Broomer ©1983 National Film Board of Canada 21 Toggling harpoon illustration by Five Seventeen 22 (inset) History Collection, Nova Scotia Museum, Halifax (detail) 22–23 Based on NSM 78.45.89, History Collection, Nova Scotia Museum, Halifax (detail) 24 Parks Canada/M84-57/Lewis Parker painting "View from a Warship—1744." Used with artist's permission (detail) 26 (Based on) Province House and Market Building. Library and Archives Canada/PA-126836 27 (Based on) Room in which Charlottetown Conference was held. Library and Archives Canada/C-021421 28 Augustine Mound, Red Bank, New Brunswick. Excavation in progress, September 11, 1975. ©Canadian Museum of Civilization, Augustine Mound, 1975, photo Dr. David Keenlyside, no. D2005-24807 (detail) 30 C. Drew Gilbert. 31 David Black, Dept. of Anthropology, University of New Brunswick (detail) 32–33 Images courtesy of Jean Bélisle, Concordia University 34 Illustration by Rick Fischer. Used with permission of the artist 35 ©William D. Finlayson 36 (Based on) Litho showing Elgin Settlement. William King/Library and Archives Canada/ e000755349 (detail) 37 Parks Canada/W.Lynch/ H.07.72.09.01(01) (detail) 38 ©Glen & Rebecca Grambo 39, 41 ©Glen & Rebecca Grambo 42 Capture of Batoche. Library and Archives Canada/C-002424 (detail) 45 C. Arnold/Prince of Wales Northern Heritage Centre 46–47 Buffalo Drive. Alfred J. Miller/Library and Archives Canada/C-000403 (detail) 49 ©Max Friesen, University of Toronto 51 Glenbow Archives NA-964-13 52 Royal British Columbia Museum, Kjerstin Mackie and Valerie Thorp examining fur garments (detail) 54, 56 ©Glen & Rebecca Grambo 57 (top) ©Canadian Museum of Civilization, artifact no. KbFk-7:308, photo Ross Taylor, image no. S90-3114 57 (bottom) ©Canadian Museum of Civilization, artifact no. 989.56.1, photo Merle Toole, image no. S90-640 58 ©Canadian Museum of Civilization, artifact no. VIII-E:51, image no. D2204-24621 64 ©Glen Grambo

NOTE: Many of the above photos and illustrations were altered by cropping, retouching, or other methods. Photos with such alterations are marked as "based on" or "detail."

Contents

Canada's Rich History   7
   Anthropology—All About Us   7
   Archaeology—More than Digging in the Dirt   7
   Archaeological Sites and Methods   8
   Historical Records   11
   Historic Sites and Living History   11
Stories of Canada   13

NEWFOUNDLAND AND LABRADOR
   L'Anse aux Meadows (Newfoundland)   14
   Port au Choix (Newfoundland)   16
   Red Bay (Labrador)   18
   L'Anse Amour (Labrador)   20
NOVA SCOTIA
   Uniacke Estate   22
   Fortress of Louisbourg   24
PRINCE EDWARD ISLAND
   Province House   26
NEW BRUNSWICK
   Augustine Mound and Oxbow Site   28
   Passamaquoddy Bay   30
QUEBEC
   Wreck of the P.S. *Lady Sherbrooke*   32
ONTARIO
   Draper Site   34
   Elgin Settlement—Buxton Historic Site   35

MANITOBA

    Prince of Wales Fort   37

NUNAVUT

    Fall Caribou Crossing, Kazan River   39

SASKATCHEWAN

    Batoche   42

NORTHWEST TERRITORIES

    Kuukpak   44

ALBERTA

    Head-Smashed-In Buffalo Jump   46

YUKON TERRITORY

    Herschel Island   49

    Dawson Historical Complex   50

BRITISH COLUMBIA

    Kwaday Dan Ts'inchi   52

    Skung Gwaii   55

Cool Treasures   57

    Sugluk Island Mask   57

    Champlain's Astrolabe   57

    Lance Point   58

Digging Up More Information   59

Index   61

About the Author   64

Canada's Rich History

What a past we have! From Viking houses to a man frozen in ice, from a gold rush boom town to an isolated island village, from everyday life thousands of years ago to voices ringing out on the road to Confederation, there are all kinds of history in Canada. And there are lots of different ways to find out about it. Let's start with the basics. Who are we and where did we come from?

Anthropology—All About Us

Anthropologists (an-throw-POL-uh-jists) are scientists who look at the whole story of humans. They study human evolution, cultures, languages, and body structures. Like time-travelling detectives, anthropologists may use clues from many places and time periods to figure out how people were alike or different. Anthropologists study living people and use facts from other sciences, such as biology and geology, to get information about our past. Some anthropologists specialize in finding out about people who lived long ago. These scientists are called archaeologists (ar-kee-OL-uh-jists) and they really "dig" history.

Archaeology—More than Digging in the Dirt

Archaeologists examine what people who lived long ago have left behind. Buildings, graves, tools, and pottery can tell archaeologists a lot about the culture, or usual way of living, of the people who made them.

Archaeological Sites and Methods

Archaeologists investigate different kinds of sites—places that show signs of the past—including burial grounds, animal kill sites, villages, and even underwater sites. The first thing archaeologists do is draw a map of the site and mark the site off into a grid of evenly spaced squares. Then they excavate, or dig up, each square and record the exact location and depth of anything they find. The archaeologists may find artifacts, which are objects made by people, or other things like bones, seeds, and ashes and charred wood from fires.

Archaelogists excavate a carefully gridded site at Kuukpak, Northwest Territories.

Archaeologists are very careful when they excavate at a site.
They don't want to destroy any information the site might hold, and
that means being very patient. Sometimes they use paintbrushes to
whisk dirt away a little at a time. Even the dirt itself can tell part of
the story. It may contain pollen—dust-sized grains produced by the
male parts of a flower—from plants that grew nearby or ground-up
rocks that were used as paints.

Archaeologists use stratigraphy (struh-TIG-ruh-fee) to determine
the age of the things they find at a site. Stratigraphy means that
newer objects are found closer to the surface than older ones. For
example, a pot found one metre down is newer than an arrowhead
from two metres down.

To find out an artifact's age in years, archaeologists use chemistry and other means. Usually, these physical tests give only a range of hundreds or thousands of years for the possible age of the artifact. Radiocarbon dating provides more accurate results for 3,000- to 4,000-year-old objects, dating them to within 60 to 100 years. This method works because living things constantly take in carbon-14 (a unique form of the carbon atom) from the atmosphere around them. But after they die, this process stops, and the carbon-14 inside them begins to change into another form of carbon called carbon-12. Scientists know the speed at which this change from carbon-14 to carbon-12 happens. By measuring the carbon-14 that's left in an object, they can tell how old it is. Archaeologists also use other clues, like the ages of similar artifacts found at other sites, to get a better idea of how old an object is.

Advances in technology have helped archaeologists find sites and record information. For example, ground-penetrating radar can show where the ground has been disturbed and even reveal buried structures. GPS (global positioning satellite) information also makes it easier to pinpoint sites and record their contents. Scientists can even feed information from digital measuring devices used at the site directly into a computer to create a three-dimensional map of the site as it gets uncovered. Later, artists may use this information to create computer-generated pictures of what a site might have looked like when people lived there.

Once an excavation is finished, there is still a lot of work to do. All the objects that have been collected must be carefully cleaned, examined, and catalogued. All the data from the site must be organized and studied. Archaeologists usually do more work in their offices and laboratories than in the field.

Historical Records

Written records like wills, diaries, and letters may contain descriptions of a site when it was active. For more recent sites, like some of those you'll be reading about, there may even be photographs filed away. Old documents may contain clues that can help archaeologists find a shipwreck.

Historic Sites and Living History

Throughout Canada, there are official historic sites recognized by the federal and provincial governments. These sites provide great opportunities to learn about an area's past. In some cases, buildings have been preserved or restored. Many of these sites feature costumed actors portraying the people who once lived there. They show what everyday life was like—what kinds of work, play, and worship took place—using replicas, or copies, of tools and toys from the past. These re-enactments bring history to life.

Herschel Island

Kuukpak

Dawson
Historical
Complex

Kwaday Dan
Ts'inchi

YUKON
TERRITORY

NORTHWEST TERRITORIES

● WHITEHORSE

● YELLOWKNIFE

Skung Gwaii

BRITISH
COLUMBIA

ALBERTA

EDMONTON ●

Batoche

● VICTORIA

Head-Smashed-In
Buffalo Jump

SASKATCHEWAN

● REGINA

Stories of Canada

Pieces of history from across Canada each tell part of our story. Let's have a look at some of them!

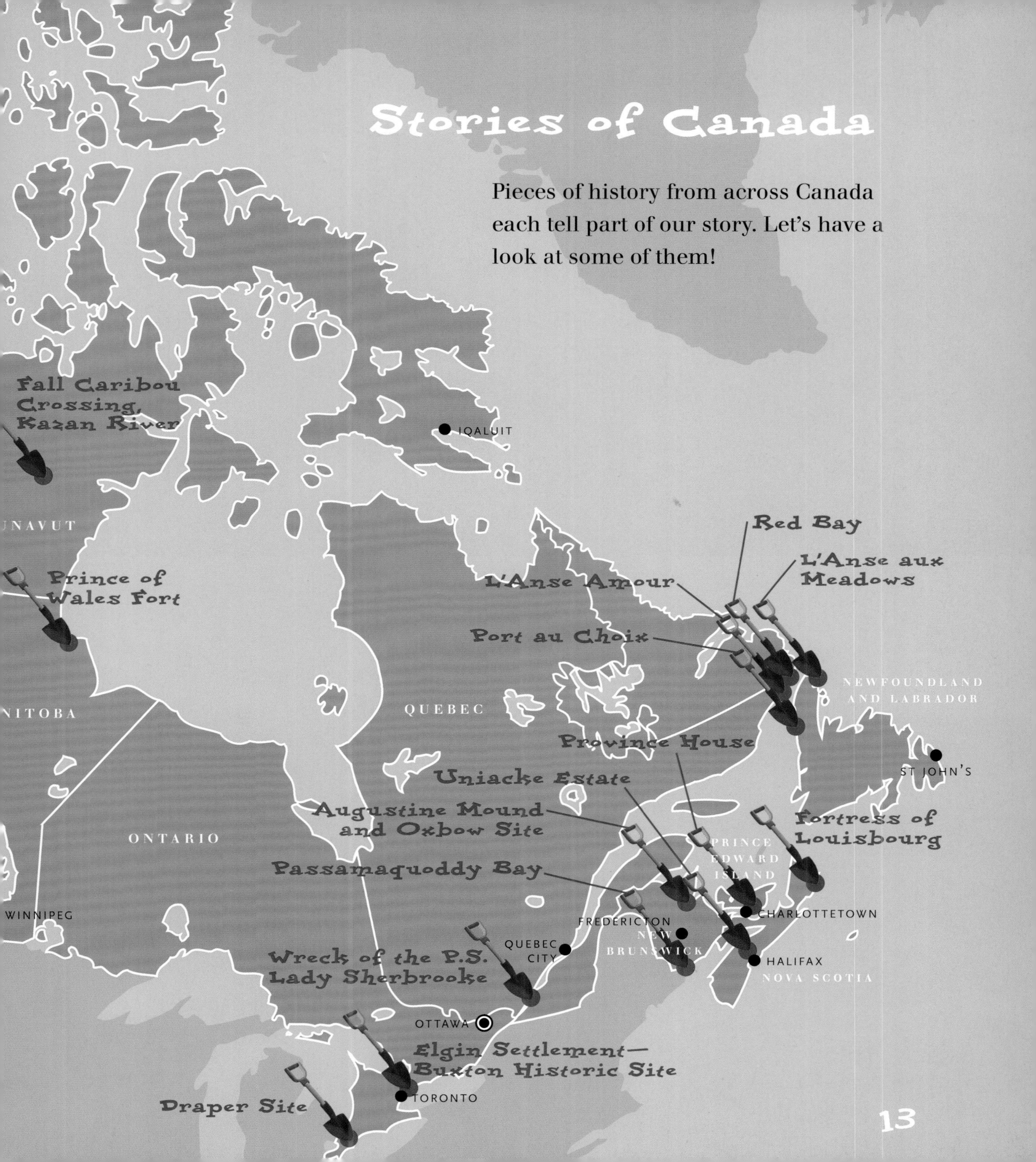

Fall Caribou Crossing, Kazan River

• IQALUIT

NUNAVUT

Prince of Wales Fort

MANITOBA

QUEBEC

L'Anse Amour

Port au Choix

Red Bay

L'Anse aux Meadows

NEWFOUNDLAND AND LABRADOR

ONTARIO

Province House

Uniacke Estate

Augustine Mound and Oxbow Site

Passamaquoddy Bay

ST JOHN'S

Fortress of Louisbourg

PRINCE EDWARD ISLAND

WINNIPEG

FREDERICTON

NEW BRUNSWICK

CHARLOTTETOWN

Wreck of the P.S. Lady Sherbrooke

QUEBEC CITY

HALIFAX

NOVA SCOTIA

◎ OTTAWA

Elgin Settlement— Buxton Historic Site

Draper Site

• TORONTO

An actor portrays a Viking blacksmith at L'Anse aux Meadows.

L'Anse aux Meadows (Newfoundland)

According to the ancient Scandinavian sagas, or stories, 30 men led by Leif Eriksson set out in a small and sleek single-sailed boat from Greenland about 1,000 years ago. After sailing west through unknown waters, these Viking explorers splashed ashore somewhere on the North American coast—about half a century before Christopher Columbus.

They found a land of lush meadows and fish-filled streams. There were forests of trees that could furnish wood for fuel and buildings—an important discovery since Greenland had no trees large enough to cut into building timbers. Liking what they saw around them, Leif's crew set up camp and stayed through the mild winter. In the spring, they sailed back to Greenland with news of this wonderful land as well as with samples of wood, grapes, and other good things they had found.

Other groups of Vikings came to see this new place called Vinland or "Land of Wine" because of the grapes Leif's men had found growing here. On one of these trips, some of the people built a small community at the head of Newfoundland's Great Northern Peninsula. No one knows how long they lived here. It could have been for only a few years, but during that time they built houses and workshops. They also built a small blacksmith's forge where they melted iron ore to produce iron in a process called smelting. The Vikings were the first people to make iron in the Americas.

Eventually, the Viking explorers began to fight with the native inhabitants of the land. Outnumbered, the Vikings packed up and went back to Greenland. The small colony they had built stood abandoned on the coast. The buildings rotted and collapsed. In time, nature took over the site again, blurring and hiding all traces of the earliest known European settlement in the New World.

Almost nine centuries later, Norwegian explorer Helge Ingstad discovered the site we now call L'Anse aux Meadows while searching for possible Viking landing places along the coast

Dig This!

L'Anse aux Meadows was first called "L'anse aux méduses"—Jellyfish Cove—by French fisherman in the 1800s. When English-speaking people saw the open meadow around the bay, they changed the pronunciation and meaning of the name.

north of New England. From 1960 to 1968, Ingstad and his archaeologist wife, Anne, led a team of archaeologists from Norway, Iceland, Sweden, and the United States as they excavated the site.

From their work, we know what the buildings, made by laying strips of sod over a wooden framework, looked like. The artifacts they found— including a spindle whorl (used in making yarn) and thread, as well as what appeared to be part of a knitting needle—told them that some of the settlers had probably been women. Other objects, such as a ringed bronze cloak pin, were like those found at Viking sites in Iceland and Greenland.

Today, a visitor to L'Anse aux Meadows can see the rebuilt Norse houses and watch costumed actors go about the tasks of daily life as the Viking settlers did a thousand years ago.

Port au Choix (Newfoundland)

Strange and frightening forces filled the world around the people. Each day brought risks and challenges. To survive, they created tools, like toggling and barbed harpoons, to improve their chances of a successful hunt. To explain and relate to the world around them, they created ideas about magic and religion. They used special objects, such as bear teeth and bird beaks, to draw upon the powers they believed in.

At Port au Choix, archaeologists have uncovered three Maritime Archaic burial sites containing more than 100 skeletons of people buried between 4,400 and 3,300 years ago. The archaeologists

A reconstruction at the visitor's centre shows what a Maritime Archaic dwelling may have looked like as well as tools like the archaeologists used to uncover the site.

Dig This!

The ancient people of Port au Choix didn't suffer much from cavities in their teeth because they didn't eat sugar. Years of eating gritty food and chewing on hides to soften them also wore down their teeth, removing the areas where cavities usually start. But sometimes their teeth wore down so much that it was quite painful.

17

Dig This!

Port au Choix looks like a French name, but it comes from the Basque name "portuichoa," which means "little harbour."

also found hundreds of artifacts, including many ornaments and magical or religious objects. One skeleton was buried with a stone carving of a killer whale. And scientists uncovered shell beads, quartz crystals, bear and wolf teeth, and the beaks and feet of birds. Port au Choix is unusual because the soil preserved organic material—bone, ivory, antler—that rots away at other sites.

The Maritime Archaic people, like those at Port au Choix, lived in Atlantic Canada and Maine from 7,500 to 3,500 years ago. They are called maritime people because they got what they needed to live from the sea. They are known as archaic (ar-KAY-ik), which means "from an earlier time," because they were hunters and gatherers rather than farmers. Hunting and gathering is the older of the two lifestyles.

Red Bay (Labrador)

Harpooning whales from small boats was a dangerous way to earn a living, but there was good money to be made if a man was brave enough. In the mid-1500s, Basque men came from their homes in the Pyrenees mountains of France and Spain to hunt whales as the animals migrated through the Strait of Belle Isle off the Labrador coast. They built a thriving industry producing whale oil, which was in great demand in Europe at that time.

Dig This!

The whalers killed more than 20,000 bowhead and right whales in only 50 years, seriously depleting the populations of both species.

As soon as someone sighted whales, the men launched their small boats from shore and set out in pursuit. If they were able to harpoon and kill a whale, they towed the carcass to shore. There, men toiled around the clock removing the blubber, or fat, chopping it into cubes, and melting it into oil in large copper pots. After the oil cooled, the men poured it into barrels and loaded the containers onto ships for transport back to Europe.

Since 1978 at Red Bay, site of the largest Basque whaling station, underwater archaeologists have found four galleons—large three-masted sailing ships—dating from the time of the whalers. They believe one of them is the *San Juan*, which sank in 1565 carrying more than 1,000 barrels of whale oil. Excavations underwater and on shore brought to light artifacts that told the story of the whaling stations and of the men who sailed to Labrador's coast each spring to risk their lives for profit.

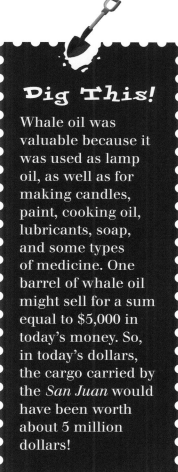

Dig This!

Whale oil was valuable because it was used as lamp oil, as well as for making candles, paint, cooking oil, lubricants, soap, and some types of medicine. One barrel of whale oil might sell for a sum equal to $5,000 in today's money. So, in today's dollars, the cargo carried by the *San Juan* would have been worth about 5 million dollars!

Wearing dive gear and using special materials for taking notes underwater, an archaeologist works on one of the galleons at Red Bay, Newfoundland.

A drawing by Steve Broomer shows what the burial ceremony at L'Anse Amour may have looked like.

L'Anse Amour (Labrador)

The people stood in a group near the grave, brought together by sorrow. The boy had died, and now all that they could do was bury him with care, leaving with him a few special possessions, including a flute made from a bird's wing bone. When the ritual was complete, the people walked away.

Now only a pile of stones hints at what happened on that day 7,500 years ago. The low, round stone burial mound at

L'Anse Amour is about nine metres wide and less than a metre high. When archaeologists first carefully removed the rocks after a road maintenance crew discovered the mound, they found a small stone chamber. The chamber was empty, but beneath it the scientists found a boy's skeleton and several artifacts that had been buried with him, including that delicate flute. There was also a spear point or knife made from a kind of rock that isn't found in the area, and a pestle, a rod-like object with a rounded end used for grinding up rocks to make paint. This pestle was made of antler.

Although we sometimes think of early people as primitive, a toggling harpoon point found in the grave shows that they used smart technology for hunting sea mammals. A normal harpoon point is permanently attached to a long pole or shaft. If the shaft broke or slipped from the hunter's hand, the harpooned animal could be lost. This toggling harpoon point slipped onto a shaft, but was also attached to a strong line, which the hunter kept in his non-throwing hand. When the hunter jabbed a seal or walrus with his harpoon, the point slid off the shaft and stuck in the animal. Hauling away on the line attached to the point, the hunter kept the animal from escaping or sinking and finally pulled it up to his boat.

A walrus tusk lying near the boy's head confirms that the L'Anse Amour people hunted these animals. The fact that the tusk was buried with the boy suggests that it meant something special to these people from long ago.

Dig This!

L'Anse Amour means "cove of love," but it's a changed pronunciation of the original name, Anse aux Morts or "cove of the dead." The place got that name because of all the shipwrecks in the area and all the lives that were lost.

A toggling harpoon like the ones used at L'Anse Amour.

21

Uniacke Estate

Imagine stepping inside from the biting cold of a Nova Scotia winter and seeing such amazing things as "5 boxes of Orange plants" and "81 pots of Geraniums"! Attorney General Richard John Uniacke's will, filed in 1830, lists all the buildings on his estate and their contents, including a hothouse and its exotic plants.

Like a greenhouse today, the hothouse was used to keep tender plants alive through Mount Uniacke's icy winters and to provide a place to start new plants early in the spring. Two very thick stone walls kept out the cold, while a fireplace heated air inside the hothouse. There was also a bark bed, which was like a giant flower box filled with tree bark instead of dirt. As it rotted, the bark gave off heat and warmed the potted plants set into the bed.

Richard John Uniacke built the hothouse on his country estate between 1813 and 1815. It has been preserved with its original furnishings, and visitors today can step back in time to experience life among Nova Scotia's 19th-century upper class.

Dig This!

A ha-ha is a deep ditch or sudden change in ground level that acts as an invisible fence. At the Uniacke estate, a ha-ha kept the sheep that grazed on a nearby hill from coming up onto the lawn around the house.

A sketch of the Uniacke Estate with a small picture [inset] showing the type of gardening that was common at the time the estate was built.

Fortress of Louisbourg

With only wilderness at their backs, 160 people stood and watched the French ship, *Semslack*, sail away, growing smaller and smaller until it disappeared altogether. Nearly all of those left behind on shore were French settlers who had built a small settlement at Plaisance (now called Placentia), Newfoundland. But France had just given Newfoundland to Britain as part of a treaty settlement so the settlers had to leave. The *Semslack* came from France to Plaisance, picked up the settlers, and brought them to this new place called Île Royale (now known as Cape Breton). Here, they would have to begin again from scratch.

The year was 1713 and the town about to be born was Louisbourg.

Although Île Royale was a popular place with fishermen from France, England, Spain, and Portugal because of the abundant cod found off its shores, no large permanent settlement took root there until the founding of Louisbourg. But only five years after the *Semslack* sailed away, Louisbourg was chosen as the capital of Île Royale, and during the next year, 1719, work began on its strong fortress.

From the time of Louisbourg's founding, the power and squabbles of distant rulers reached across the Atlantic to affect the lives of the settlers and soldiers living there. As wars came and went in Europe, foreign soldiers attacked, besieged, and even took over Louisbourg. Finally, in 1760, the British destroyed the city's fortifications.

Today, you can walk through an amazingly detailed reconstruction of Louisbourg. With the help of skilled labourers, archaeologists, and historians, the Government of Canada has reconstructed one-fifth of the fortified town. Actors in costumes bring Louisbourg's history to life—life in an 18th-century French fortress, that is!

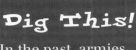

Dig This!

In the past, armies attacking fortified towns often used an ancient tactic known as siege (SEEJ). The army would besiege (bee-SEEJ) the town by surrounding it and cutting it off from the outside. The town would often be forced to surrender when it ran out of food or water.

Dig This!

People in Louisbourg changed clothes regularly and washed their faces and hands, but they probably took a bath only once or twice a year. People at that time thought that the oil on their bodies helped to keep them healthy.

Province House sits squarely behind the round Market Building in this early photograph of Charlottetown.

PRINCE EDWARD ISLAND

Province House

Trick riders, trained monkeys, and performing ponies!! In the autumn of 1864, the Slaymaker and Nichols Circus performed for four days in Charlottetown, Prince Edward Island. People travelled from all over the island and from other places in the Maritimes to see the shows. The politicians taking part in a conference at the same time found the streets of the normally quiet city crowded and noisy. Busy with finding a place to stay and getting settled, the men probably still found time to think about the importance of their upcoming meetings. In fact, this gathering would shape the future of Canada.

In the 1860s, British Columbia, Newfoundland, Nova Scotia, New Brunswick, Prince Edward Island, and the Province of Canada (which became Ontario and Quebec after Confederation) were all British colonies. For years, there had been proposals for uniting these colonies into one new country, including one from Richard John Uniacke of Nova Scotia. (Remember reading about his estate earlier?) The maritime colonies finally set a date and place—September 1, 1864, at a building called Province House—for a conference on their union. The leaders of the Province of Canada asked to participate, and from that conference came the first real progress toward the creation of Canada. For that reason, Province House is known as the birthplace of Confederation.

The room where those discussions took place has been restored to look as it did in 1864. And history is still being made at Province House: the Prince Edward Island legislature meets there and has done so since 1847.

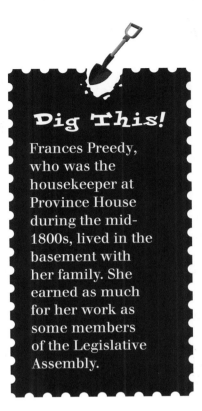

Dig This!

Frances Preedy, who was the housekeeper at Province House during the mid-1800s, lived in the basement with her family. She earned as much for her work as some members of the Legislative Assembly.

The room in which the Charlottetown Conference was held.

Augustine Mound, Red Bank, New Brunswick. Excavation in progress, September 11, 1975.

Augustine Mound and Oxbow Site

Good fishing encouraged the ancestors of the Miramichi Mi'kmaq to settle in Metepenagiag, now known as Red Bank, nearly 3,000 years ago. In the 1970s, one of their descendents, Red Bank First Nation Elder Joseph Augustine, made an exciting find when he discovered an ancient burial mound in the area. Curious about their community's ancient past, members of the Red Bank First Nation worked with archaeologists to learn more.

Carefully, the scientists excavated the mound, which is circular and measures about 11.5 metres across and one metre high. They found human remains that had been buried with tools, weapons, and ornaments, including thousands of copper beads. Many objects foreign to New Brunswick, such as pipes made of Ohio clay, told of a people who had come from afar. The site, which was built about 2,400 years ago, is a sacred place to the Mi'kmaq and treated with great respect.

Digging at various other sites in the Red Bank area revealed alternating dark and light layers. The dark layers, made of organic material such as food debris and charcoal from fires, came from times when people lived on the site. The light layers were made of sand left behind when the river flooded the area in the spring. The archaeologists found many artifacts, including stone arrowheads, pieces of clay cooking pots, and stone knives.

The largest ancient site at Red Bank is the Oxbow site, which is about as long as two football fields and has a 2-metre-thick history-holding layer. Over the years, many groups of people from the region occupied this popular seasonal fishing place.

Dig This!

Red Bank is the oldest continuously occupied community in New Brunswick.

Dig This!

The oldest woven fabric known to have been made in Atlantic Canada, believed to be about 2,500 years old, was found in the mound Augustine discovered.

Passamaquoddy Bay

By looking through your garbage, someone could learn a lot about you and your family. Heaps of discarded shells along the shores of Passamaquoddy (pass-uh-muh-ᴋᴡᴏᴅ-ee) Bay in southern New Brunswick tell archaeologists a lot about the people who lived there over the last few thousand years. These garbage heaps, known as middens, contain the bones of deer, beaver, muskrat, seal, cod, and sturgeon as well as many kinds of shellfish, such as horse mussels and scallops.

Because winters were mild along the bay and food was abundant, people settled here during the winter. They dug their houses into the ground, which helped to keep out the weather. When the tide went out, they gathered shellfish along the beaches, throwing the shells onto piles near their houses. These are the middens we see today. Archaeologists have found hundreds of these sites along the bay.

Dig This!

Scallop draggers are boats that drag bags made of metal rings along the ocean floor to scoop up shellfish. In Passamaquoddy Bay, scallop draggers have pulled up half-moon-shaped slate knives from the ocean floor. About 6,000 to 7,000 years old, these knives look a lot like Arctic Inuit ulus (oo-loos) and were probably used for much the same thing: skinning and butchering seals. Archaeologists think that seal hunters may have lost the knives out on the ice. When the ice melted, the knives dropped to the sea floor.

This knife with a blade made from a beaver's front tooth was found at one of the midden sites.

A midden may look like a pile of dirt, shells, and bone bits but it can tell us a lot about what early people ate.

Wreck of the P.S. Lady Sherbrooke

On July 30, 1817, the Paddlewheel Steamer (P.S.) *Lady Sherbrooke* built up steam in her boilers and left Hart Logan's shipyard behind to carry passengers and cargo on the St. Lawrence River. Part of John Molson's fleet, she was one of the first steamships to operate on the St. Lawrence. The use of steam engines was revolutionary because it allowed shipping companies to set and keep schedules. When the ships relied on sail power, the trip from Montreal to Quebec City could take as little as 15 hours or more than 2 weeks. Imagine trying to figure out when goods or people would arrive!

Less than 10 years after her launch, her owners retired the *Lady Sherbrooke*. Workers removed her steam engine, which was placed on a new ship, and a boat towed her to the shallow waters off Ile Charon near the Molson family summer home. Men cut a hole in the bottom of her hull and scuttled, or sank, her. Over the years, silt and sand drifted over the wreck. After that, no one thought much about the

Lady Sherbrooke until in the 1970s the Comité d'Histoire et d'Archéologie Subaquatique du Québec proposed excavating her.

Finding and excavating an underwater site isn't an easy job. Scientists first used a sonar survey, which measures how sounds bounce off different objects, to map the area where the ship was believed to lie and to pinpoint the most likely place for excavation. Once the site was located, they arranged for a research boat and all the equipment that would be needed for the project to be brought to the location. Over nine seasons, divers worked on the site.

A cutaway view of the Lady Sherbrooke is shown below. Above is a photograph of a chessman found during the excavation.

Underwater archaeologists map a site and record the position of artifacts just like archaeologists working on land. But strong currents, muddy water that makes it hard to see, and the limited air supply in divers' tanks can make their job more difficult.

Dig This!

Cargo hauled on a single trip by the *Lady Sherbrooke* in 1820 might include over 500 barrels of flour, 25 barrels of butter, and 15 barrels of pork. There would also be some casks of cider and baskets of bottles. Add to this some odds and ends such as a desk, a sawhorse, and three beds. Some small packages, as well as boxes and kegs of various goods, would be tucked into the remaining spaces in the hold.

Draper Site

Dig This!

The Huron peoples originally lived in villages along the St. Lawrence River and around the Great Lakes. Their longhouses had a bark covering placed over a framework of poles. Each house was about 6 metres wide, about 4.5 to 6 metres tall, and ranged from about 12 to 76 metres long. The length of the house depended on the number of families living in it.

A computer recreation of the Draper Site by artist Rick Fischer.

In 1975, a crew of from 10 to 60 students at a time worked for six months to explore the site of a 500-year-old Huron village before it was scheduled to be destroyed to make way for new construction. With the careful use of bulldozers and road graders, archaeologists were able to excavate five acres of the area, known as the Draper site.

Construction can be a blessing or a curse to archaeologists. Construction activities can uncover new sites for archaeologists to investigate, or obliterate sites forever. The Draper site was on land intended to become part of the new Toronto International Airport at Pickering, the reason why the archaeologists made such an effort. They were able to relax a bit after six months of intense work because the construction was cancelled. Excavation continued at a slower pace over the next several years.

Part of a pipe found at the Draper Site shows a human face.

The investigation uncovered more than 200,000 pieces of clay pots, thousands of clay pipe fragments, and thousands of stone artifacts. The archaeologists also found the remains of 34 Huron dwellings called longhouses.

Elgin Settlement —Buxton Historic Site

Before the American Civil War, slaves fleeing north to freedom often travelled all the way into Canada. For many, the Elgin Settlement was the last station on the Underground Railroad.

Reverend William King founded Elgin in 1849 and supervised it as it grew to a community of 1,200 to 2,000 people. Farming was the main business, but the town also had a sawmill, brickyard, blacksmith shop, and dry goods store. Believing education for themselves and their children was very important, the Elgin settlers set up two excellent schools.

The success of Elgin and other Black Canadian settlements showed that Black people could succeed after slavery. It seems strange now to think anyone would need to be shown this, but in those times the beliefs of many people were different.

Dig This!

A dry goods store sold such things as fabrics, clothes, and buttons.

Dig This!

The Underground Railroad was the name given to a secret organization that helped slaves flee from the southern United States to safe places. In many areas of the United States, it was a crime to help escaped slaves.

A drawing of the Elgin settlement from a pamphlet written by its founder, William King.

MANITOBA

Prince of Wales Fort

Life at Prince of Wales Fort wasn't very pleasant. In the winter, it was very cold, and even roaring wood fires in the stoves couldn't keep things from freezing indoors. And unfortunately the fires made it smoky. In the summer, blackflies and mosquitoes made the men miserable. However, they were eager to work here because they could earn a good salary.

In 1689, the Hudson's Bay Company (HBC) set up a trading post at the mouth of the Churchill River. They wanted to trade with the Dene, Inuit, and Cree peoples living in the area. The trading post burned that same year, but in 1717 the HBC built

An aerial view of the fort shows the arrow-shaped bastion points that let cannon fire be directed back along the fort's walls if attackers came in close. The wide V of stone in front of the fort is called a ravelin and protects the main gate from direct attack.

Dig This!

Depending on when they visit, tourists to Prince of Wales Fort may see polar bears or beluga whales.

on the site again. By 1730, the situation between England and France became tense, and the HBC decided that building a stone fortress would be a good way to protect their trading ships and their Royal Navy escorts. A stone fortress would also discourage French fur traders from coming into the area.

The fortress took more than 40 years to build. The design, known as a bastion (BASS-chun) fort, allowed fire from the stronghold's 40 cannons to be directed back along the base of each wall if necessary. It took very long to finish the construction because the men spent a lot of their time doing the things they needed to do to survive: chopping wood, hunting food, hauling water, and trading for fur.

In 1783, the French captured the fort without firing a single shot. They burned the buildings inside the fort, set off explosives in the cannons to wreck them, and blew up parts of the outer walls. Prince of Wales Fort was eventually returned to the British, but it lay abandoned and in ruins until the 1930s, when the Canadian government began to restore it.

Forty cannons like this one supplied the firepower for the fort.

Travelling south to the treeline for the winter, a barren ground caribou herd crosses a stream.

NUNAVUT

Fall Caribou Crossing, Kazan River

The land seemed to be alive. Thousands and thousands of caribou moved in endless waves, packed so tightly that one couldn't see the ground between them. The animals at the front of the herd hesitated at the river's edge, looking for a shallow or narrow place to cross, and then plunged ahead. Pushed by the mass of animals behind them, scrambling over slippery rocks and struggling against the current, the swimming caribou had no attention to spare for the men paddling kayaks toward them.

Dig This!

The last time caribou were hunted from kayaks on the Kazan River was probably in the 1950s or 1960s.

Caribou were the heart of life to the inland Inuit. From them came food, shelter, clothing, fuel, and tools. Forming the largest migration of land animals on earth, caribou travel in an endless circle between spring calving grounds in the north and the winter shelter of the treeline in the south.

Each fall, the Inuit gathered at certain places along the Kazan River and at other locations where the caribou crossed water to continue their journey. Hunters in kayaks used spears to kill as many of the swimming animals as possible.

After the hunt, the caribou were skinned and butchered. Women prepared the skins to be used as clothing, which they later sewed. Meat was cached (cashed)—or stored for later—when the caribou had moved on. Caches were covered with plenty of rocks to keep animals from getting at the meat. An upright rock was placed nearby to help in locating the cache even when it was covered in snow.

In 1992, Inuit elders began working with archaeologists to record the way of life at the caribou crossing. As a result of their efforts, 30 kilometres along the river from Kazan Falls to the east end of Thirty Mile Lake were set aside as a historic site—a place central to the life of a people.

Caribou cows and calves find a narrow crossing point.

Batoche

Dig This!

Riel's trial and execution created hard feelings between Quebec and English-speaking Canada, and they continue to influence politics today.

The fighting at Batoche (ba-TAHSH) lasted only four days, but what happened here in 1885 had an effect on Canada that lasted long after the guns fell silent.

Founded in the early 1870s by Metis (MAY-tee) settlers from Manitoba, the village of Batoche grew up around a ferry crossing that merchant and farmer Xavier "Batoche" Letendre built on the banks of the South Saskatchewan River. By 1885, about 500 people lived in the small town.

In the early 1880s, the Metis and many First Nation peoples were unhappy with how the Canadian government was treating them. In 1884, the Saskatchewan Metis asked Louis Riel, who had led the Metis against the government in Manitoba in 1870, to come from Montana and lead them in their struggle.

In March 1885, after failed attempts to negotiate land claims with the government, Riel established a provisional government at Batoche. He named himself President and Gabriel Dumont military commander. Armed conflict soon followed, at first with the North West Mounted Police and then with the government troops of the North West Field Force, commanded by General Middleton.

It was Middleton's attack on Riel's base at Batoche that brought the uprising to an end. On the fourth day of fighting, May 12, 1885, Middleton's 800 troops broke through the Metis lines. Riel and Dumont escaped, but others were captured and held for trial. The back of the Northwest Rebellion was broken, and Riel gave himself up three days later. He was tried for treason, found guilty, and hanged in Regina, Saskatchewan, on November 16, 1885.

Dig This!

Metis are people whose ancestry is traced back to unions between women of the Ojibway, Cree, or Saulteaux First Nations and European fur traders, usually French or Scottish men.

An artist's depiction titled "The Capture of Batoche" was supposedly based on sketches made during the fighting.

Kuukpak

The elders of the Inuvialuit (ee-new-vee-AH-loo-eet) keep the history of their people. When the elders saw that waves and ice might one day erode the remains of an ancient village built by their ancestors, they decided to tell archaeologists what they knew about it. The elders asked the archaeologists to look at the site and uncover what they could about its past.

Dig This!

European whalers, traders, and missionaries brought diseases like smallpox to the Kuukpangmiut and other northern peoples. These illnesses took a terrible toll on the native peoples because they had no immunity, or resistance, to them. Many communities were nearly or completely wiped out.

Hundreds of years ago, the ancestors of the Inuvialuit lived along the Mackenzie River and were called the Kuukpangmiut (kook-PANG-mee-oot)—people of the great river. Kuukpak (KOOK-pahk), or "great river," referred to the Mackenzie and was also the name of a Kuukpangmiut village located near the coast of Qangmaliq (KANG-mah-leek) Bay. Here, the people spent their summers hunting beluga whales and stockpiling meat for the winter.

The Kuukpangmiut lived in houses built of driftwood covered with sod. Shifting soil buried most of these dwellings long ago. Excavating in the permanently frozen ground wasn't easy, but the permafrost had preserved material that might otherwise have rotted away. Archaeologists unearthed enough of a driftwood house to allow them to reconstruct what it must have looked like.

In many cases, the archaeologists turned to the elders to find out what an artifact might be and how it would have been used. For example, a shallow stone bowl with a ridge inside was actually a lamp. It would have been filled with seal or whale blubber and held a wick made of moss or cotton grass.

Bit by bit, the house at Kuukpak is uncovered from its chilly resting place.

Head-Smashed-In Buffalo Jump

Before the Spanish explorers brought horses to the New World, killing a bison, which could weigh more than 800 kilograms and could run 50 kilometres an hour, would have been very difficult and dangerous. But bison were as essential to the people of the plains as caribou were to the people of the north. These great animals,

Driving bison over a cliff was an efficient way to kill many of them at once, whether the hunters were on foot or on horseback as in this painting by Alfred J. Miller.

which are also referred to as buffalo, furnished food, clothing, and shelter. Buffalo jumps were a clever and well-planned solution to the problem of killing enough bison while staying safe.

Good grazing near the buffalo jump naturally attracted the animals. The people built drive lanes—rows of stone piles or cairns—that helped to funnel the animals toward the cliff kill site. At Head-Smashed-In, there are more than 500 of these stone cairns in drive lanes that start 10 kilometres west of the cliff.

The hunt began when young men called "Buffalo Runners" made the sound of a lost buffalo calf, luring the herd leaders to follow them towards drive lanes. Once the animals neared the lanes, the men circled behind the herd and upwind of them. They yelled and flapped hides or robes. Frightened, the animals rushed forward, the thunder of their hooves shaking the ground. When the herd reached the cliff, the bison in front tried to stop, but the stampeding animals behind them forced them over the cliff.

At the bottom of the 10- to 18-metre cliff, more people waited to finish off the dying animals and to butcher the dead bison. Much of the meat was made into pemmican by drying it and then pounding it together with grease, bone marrow, and berries. Pemmican was a high-calorie food that could be stored for quite a long time.

Head-Smashed-In was used by the aboriginal people of the plains for at least 5,700 years, right up until the mid-1800s. In the bone piles at the base of the cliff, which are 10 metres thick in some places, archaeologists have found worn or broken stone tools, stone knives, dart points, and arrowheads. The hunters camped nearby on a large flat area, and the remains of a few teepee rings can still be seen. Archaeologists have uncovered a kilometre-wide area that holds the remains of cooking pits and meat caches.

The excavation on Herschel Island revealed the remains of a 1,000-year-old house.

YUKON TERRITORY

Herschel Island

Day after day, year after year, waves smashed against the shore of Herschel Island, relentlessly eating away at the land and the ancient remains of a dwelling that once stood there. Before the site was completely destroyed, archaeologists excavated it and found that it was built about 1,000 years ago.

At about that time, a new people appeared in Arctic Canada. The Thule (TOO-lee) came from Alaska and would eventually spread all the way to the eastern coast of Canada. One of the first places they stopped appears to have been Herschel Island, or Qikiqtaruk (kee-KEEK-tah-ruk), as their

Inuvialuit descendants call it. They were probably attracted to the area by the abundant fish and game.

The Thule ate seal, but they also hunted bowhead whales from their skin-covered kayaks (KYE-acks)—enclosed one-man boats—and umiaqs (oo-mee-acks)—open boats that could carry 10 to 12 people. They used dogs to pull sleds with runners made of whalebone. Thule houses were partially dug into the gravel beaches and built of sod-covered driftwood frames. Some of the villages may have held as many as 200 people.

Two other houses on Herschel Island have been dated to about 500 years ago. Near the houses, archaeologists found middens and the remains of what was probably a rack for preparing bowhead whale meat for storage.

Dawson Historical Complex

Psst! Did you hear there's gold in the Yukon? At the turn of the 20th century, the rush was on and Dawson City became a boom town. Some prospectors pitched their tents near the city's waterfront. Others just passed through on their way to the goldfields. The town offered a post office, a steam laundry, saloons, banks where the prospectors could exchange their gold for cash, and stores selling everything from dry goods to hardware. You could buy anything, from a stetson cowboy hat to Fry's cocoa, but you paid Dawson prices. Eggs sold for 30 cents a dozen elsewhere in Canada. In Dawson, they would set you back anywhere from $2 to $18. Gold rush Dawson had social events and celebrations but also shootings and attempted bank robberies. It was definitely a lively place!

THE CANADIAN BANK OF COMM
CAPITAL PAID UP SIX MILLION DOLLA

SHIPMENT OF GOLD DUST. SEPT-20-99. #750,000.00   GOETZMAN. DAWSON

Dig This!

Robert W. Service, the Canadian poet who wrote great stories about the gold rush days, worked in a bank in Dawson around that time.

A $750,000 gold shipment leaves a Dawson City bank on September 20, 1899.

Some of the buildings from this era have been restored and offer visitors a glimpse of Dawson's hectic past. You can imagine the post office filled with people mailing money orders home to their families, or waiting outside in the winter for the mail to arrive by dogsled. Maybe your mind can conjure up what it must have been like on the dirt streets when it rained or the snow melted. Think of the smells and sounds of crowds of people and animals in the bug-filled summertime. And imagine the excitement when someone made a new discovery—gold!

Textile conservators, Kjerstin Mackie and Valerie Thorp examine the fur garments of Kwaday Dan Ts'inchi at the Royal British Columbia Museum.

BRITISH COLUMBIA

Kwaday Dan Ts'inchi

For 550 years, he lay as though asleep, covered in a blanket of ice and snow. Then, one day in 1999, three schoolteachers hunting mountain sheep high in Tatshenshini-Alsek Provincial Park noticed a walking stick lying in a melting glacier. Then they saw fur and bits of bone. At first they thought it was the remains of an animal. Then they noticed the clothing, some of it with stitching.

The hunters realized that they had found something extraordinary, something very old. Leaving the remains untouched, they put a few artifacts into a plastic bag and hiked back down the mountain to tell someone about what they had discovered. An archaeologist then called the Champagne and Aishihik First Nations, who claim the land where the remains came to light. They helped to organize the team that went back by helicopter to investigate the site.

The team found that the body was in two main pieces: the upper body with the left arm attached but the head and right arm missing, and the lower body with the lower legs and feet missing. Nearby were several artifacts, including a wooden dart, a walking stick, a knife still in its sheath, a woven hat, and some tattered pieces of clothing. The scientists also found what appeared to be a "medicine bag" containing items that would have held special powers and meaning for the man. Considered sacred, this medicine bag was left unopened.

The remains of the man, who was given the name Kwaday Dan Ts'inchi (kwuh-DAY dun SIN-chee) meaning "Long Ago Person Found," were taken to the Royal British Columbia Museum for study. The scientists were given only a year to examine the remains, which they preserved in a locked freezer, before they were returned to the Champagne and Aishihik First Nations for reburial. Out of respect for Kwaday, the museum released no photographs of his body. Kwaday's remains were cremated, and his ashes scattered to the winds at the place where he was found. It's still a mystery where he came from, why he was there, and where he was going.

Dig This!

In many places, climate change is helping to reveal the past. Artifacts and sites are being uncovered on the tundra and in the mountains as glaciers melt and permafrost thaws.

Skung Gwaii

After a rough ride on the open ocean, it's a relief to reach the shelter of the tree-lined cove. Along the shore, a few totem poles and mortuary poles reach up like ghostly fingers through a low mist. Mortuary poles were built to hold the remains of a dead person, usually wealthy, in a grave box near the top. Near the poles, great cedar logs that once made up huge longhouses lie as if sleeping under thick blankets of moss.

Known to the Haida people as Skung Gwaii (skung gwy), this remote World Heritage Site is an amazing place—the only place in the world with the remains of a traditional Northwest Coast village. Also called Anthony Island, it lies at the southern tip of the Queen Charlotte Islands or Haida Gwaii (HIDE-uh gwy), as the Haida refer to them.

Home to the Haida people, the islands of Haida Gwaii provide a lush environment full of abundant food and resources. This gave the people who lived there time to develop a rich and complex society, filled with art and ceremony. They carved elaborate house fronts and totem poles that told those who saw them about the families who owned them. At the time the first Europeans reached Haida Gwaii, which means "islands of the people," there were at least 50 thriving villages throughout the islands.

Many poles were removed from the site at various times, some with the permission of the Haida people, some without. Scientists are working with the Haida

Haida totem poles still stand looking out to sea on Skung Gwaii.

Dig This!

A portion of the southern part of Haida Gwaii has been set aside as Gwaii Haanas (gwy HAH-nahz) National Park Reserve /Haida Historic Site. This area, which includes Skung Gwaii, holds an abundance of natural and historic treasures.

to help preserve the poles still standing at Skung Gwaii. Because the Haida will allow only certain measures to be taken, the poles will eventually decay and fall, which is part of the natural cycle of the islands. Archaeologists are working to record as much information as possible before that happens.

A carved face from one of the Skung Gwaii totem poles.

Cool Treasures

There have been some truly amazing objects brought to light from Canada's past!

Sugluk Island Mask

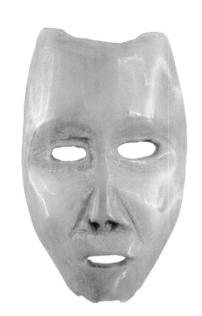

This tiny ivory mask—only 35 mm tall and 20 mm wide—was found during the excavation of a 2,000-year-old village on Sugluk Island, Nunavut, in Hudson Strait near the northwest coast of Labrador.

Champlain's Astrolabe

From ancient times up until the late 1500s, mariners used astrolabes to find their position by measuring the height of the sun and certain stars above the horizon. This one was found on a little-known route taken by the French explorer Samuel de Champlain in June 1613 as he made his way up the Ottawa River. Although there's no way to prove the astrolabe was actually Champlain's, it probably did belong to him. No one else who might have owned such a device is known to have followed this route at that time.

Lance Point

Between 3,000 and 5,000 years ago, someone took a piece of copper they found and hammered it into this 12-cm-long spear or lance point. Copper is an unusual metal because it's sometimes found in its "native" or pure form rather than mixed in with minerals that have to be processed to release the metal. Native copper was often found, used, and traded by the people living along the shores of the Great Lakes. This point came from a site near Hull, Quebec.

Digging Up More Information

Libraries and museums offer lots of information about archaeology, anthropology, and history. Provincial archives have photographs, letters, and all kinds of other historic data about each province's people and past. Just dig in! Or try these sites online:

Four Great Places to Begin Your Excavations

The Canadian Museum of Civilization
www.civilization.ca

The Virtual Museum of Canada
www.virtualmuseum.ca

Canadian History and Heritage @ culture.ca
www.culture.ca/explore-explorez-e.jsp?category=500

Parks Canada—National Historic Sites
www.pc.gc.ca/progs/lhn-nhs/

Sites About Places in This Book

Newfoundland—L'Anse aux Meadows
www.pc.gc.ca/lhn-nhs/nl/meadows/

Newfoundland—Port au Choix
www.pc.gc.ca/lhn-nhs/nl/portauchoix/

Labrador—Red Bay
www.civilization.ca/hist/canp1/ca04eng.html

Labrador—L'Anse Amour
www.labradorstraits.net/home/16

Nova Scotia—Uniacke Estate
museum.gov.ns.ca/arch/sites/uniacke/

Nova Scotia—Fortress of Louisbourg

collections.ic.gc.ca/louisbourg/

Prince Edward Island—Province House (and Confederation)

www.pc.gc.ca/lhn-nhs/pe/provincehouse/natcul/natcul1_e.asp

www.collectionscanada.ca/confederation/

New Brunswick—Oxbow Site and Augustine Mound

collections.ic.gc.ca/oxbow/

New Brunswick—Passamaquoddy Bay

www.civilization.ca/hist/lifelines/licrn01e.html

Quebec—Wreck of the P.S. *Lady Sherbrooke*

collections.ic.gc.ca/lady/

Ontario—Elgin Settlement/Buxton Historic Site

www.buxtonmuseum.com

Manitoba—Prince of Wales Fort

www.pc.gc.ca/lhn-nhs/mb/prince/

Saskatchewan—Batoche

www.pc.gc.ca/lhn-nhs/sk/batoche/

Northwest Territories—Kuukpak

pwnhc.learnnet.nt.ca/exhibits/kuukpak/

Alberta—Head-Smashed-In Buffalo Jump

www.head-smashed-in.com

Yukon Territory—Herschel Island

www.virtualmuseum.ca/Exhibitions/Herschel/

Yukon Territory—Dawson City

www.pc.gc.ca/lhn-nhs/yt/dawson/

British Columbia—Kwaday Dan Ts'inchi

srmwww.gov.bc.ca/arch/kwaday/

British Columbia—Skung Gwaii

www.virtualmuseum.ca/Exhibitions/Haida/java/english/gh/gh2.html

Index

A

Alberta   12, 46–48, 60
Anthony Island   55
anthropology   7
archaeological methods   8, 9, 10, 19
archaeological sites   8, 9, 10
archaeology   7
artifacts   8, 9, 10
astrolabe   57
Augustine, Joseph   28
Augustine Mound   13, 28–29, 60

B

Basque   18
bastion fort   37, 38
baths   25
Batoche   12, 42–43, 60
beluga whales   38, 44
bison   46–48
Blackfoot   48
bowhead whales   18, 49, 50
British Columbia   12, 52–56, 60
buffalo   47
Buffalo Runners   48
bulldozers   35
Buxton Historic Site   13, 35–36, 60

C

Cape Breton   13, 24
caribou   39–41
Champagne and Aishihik First
  Nations   53
Champlain, Samuel de   57

Champlain's Astrolabe   57
Charlottetown   13, 26, 27
Churchill River   37
Civil War   35
Confederation   26–27, 60
copper   29, 58
Cree   37

D

Dawson Historical Complex   12,
  50–51, 60
Dene   37
disease   44, 56
Draper Site   13, 34–35
dry goods store   36
Dumont, Gabriel   43

E

Elgin Settlement   13, 35–36, 60
Eriksson, Leif   14, 15

F

fabric   29
Fall Caribou Crossing   13, 39–41

G

galleon   19
gold rush   50
Greenland   14
Gwaii Haanas National Park
  Reserve   55

H

ha-ha   23
Haida Gwaii   55
harpoon   21
Head-Smashed-In Buffalo
  Jump   12, 46–48, 60
Herschel Island   12, 49–50, 60
Hudson's Bay Company   37, 38
Huron   34, 35
hothouse   22

I

Île Charon   32
Île Royale   24
Ingstad, Helge   15, 16
Inuit   30, 37, 40
Inuvialuit   44, 50

J

Jellyfish Cove   15

K

kayaks   39, 40, 50
Kazan River   39, 40
King, William   36
Kuukpak   12, 44–45, 60
Kuukpangmiut   44
Kwaday Dan Ts'inchi   12, 52–53, 60

L

Labrador   13, 18–21, 59
Lady Sherbrooke   13, 32–33, 60
Lance Point   59
L'Anse Amour   13, 20–21, 59
L'Anse aux Meadows   13, 14–16, 59
Letendre, Xavier   43
longhouse   34, 35, 55
Louisbourg   13, 24–25, 60

M

Mackenzie River   44
Manitoba   13, 37–38, 60
Maritime Archaic   16, 17, 18
medicine bag   53
Metepenagiag   28
Metis   43
middens   30, 50
Middleton, General   43
Mi'kmaq   28
Molson, John   32

N

New Brunswick   13, 28–31, 60
Newfoundland   13, 14–18, 59
Northwest Rebellion   43
Northwest Territories   12, 44–45, 60
Nova Scotia   13, 22–25, 59, 60
Nunavut   12–13, 39–41, 57

O

Ontario   13, 34–36, 60
Oxbow Site   13, 29, 60

P

Passamaquoddy Bay   13, 30–31, 60
pemmican   48
permafrost   44, 53
Plaisance   24
polar bears   38
Port aux Choix   13, 16–18, 59
Preedy, Frances   27
Prince Edward Island   13, 26–27, 60
Prince of Wales Fort   13, 37–38, 60
Province House   13, 26–27, 60
Province of Canada   27

Q

Qangmaliq   44
Qikiqtaruk   50
Quebec   32–33
Queen Charlotte Islands   55

R

radiocarbon dating   10
Red Bank   28, 29
Red Bay   13, 18–19, 59
Riel, Louis   42, 43
right whales   18

S

San Juan   19
Saskatchewan   12, 42–43, 60
scallop draggers   30
Semslack   24, 25
Service, Robert   51
Sherbrooke, Sir John Coape   32
Sherbrooke, Katherine   32
siege   25
Skung Gwaii   12, 54–56, 60
slaves   35, 36
steam engines   32
St. Lawrence River   32, 34
stratigraphy   9
Sugluk Island Mask   57

T

Tatshenshini-Alsek Provincial
  Park   52
Thirty Mile Lake   40
Thule   49, 50
trading post   37

U

ulus   30
umiaqs   50
Underground Railroad   35, 36
underwater site   35, 36
Uniacke Estate   13, 22–23, 59
Uniacke, Richard   22, 27

V

Vikings   14–16
Vinland   15

W

whale oil   18, 19
World Heritage Site   16, 55

Y

Yukon Territory   12, 49–50, 60

About the Author

Rebecca L. Grambo is the award-winning author of more than
20 books for adults and children. Her recent titles include *Digging
Canadian Dinosaurs*, *Lupé: A Wolf Cub's First Year*, and *Wolf: Legend,
Enemy, Icon*. She lives in Warman, Saskatchewan, with her husband,
Glen, and a house full of rabbits, chinchillas, guinea pigs, and rats.
She loves visiting historic places and antique stores.